WISDOM RUN

INSIGHTS INTO A SMALL PLANET

Gregory L. Schroer

Wisdom Run
Insights into a Small Planet

Gregory L. Schroer

Wisdom
knowledge, learning, evolution

Run
*to go, move, grow
easily and freely
without hindrance or restraint*

Copyright © 2014 Gregory L. Schroer
All rights reserved.

ISBN: 0692236643
ISBN 13: 9780692236642
Library of Congress Control Number: 2014911070
Wisdom Run, Clovis, California

Cover and interior photographs copyrighted © by Gregory L. Schroer.
Title, text and poems copyrighted © by Gregory L. Schroer,
except for the poem by Lama Govinda on page 81.
We gratefully acknowledge the use of his poem in this book.

The author can be reached by email at:
greg.schroer@gmail.com; and wisdomrun.com.

To

those who seek and appreciate

the natural and cultural beauty

found within our small planet.

What is the human condition without inspiration?

*Inspiration can easily be lost, or maybe never found,
as we live busy lives, or possibly even
living a life of quiet desperation.*

*But we have a choice to make during our short lives,
including taking time to appreciate
the world around us.*

*Come into this journey.
It is more than what you see; it is also how you feel.
And more than a celebration; it is a search
to drill down into and not to pass over.*

*With quiet openness and reflection, this journey
too can bring you a breath of fresh air,
and maybe even bring greater inspiration
into your world.*

Journey

I. Reflections

II. Pacific Inspiration

III. Pursuing the Essence Within

I

Reflections

*C*ome home...

to these

wide-open spaces

Where the earth

and mind

breathe free

Give me light...

Give me time

Give me many lives

to see

the sublime...

Bring me your passion
    your reflective grace
        your depth of centeredness
            your measured pace

Bring me your strength
    your steady gait
        your calming pace
            your destined fate

Bring me your peace
    your quiet days
        your lasting friendship
            your gentle ways

Bring me home
    to the softening light
        into the calmness
            of a darkening night

*S*eek the serene places
the places that inspire
places with integrity
of the ages
made by forces
much greater and
longer lived
than our own

Here is the foundation
the solid
grounded base

On this vulnerable
floating mass

we call home

Beckoning within

yearning beyond

It is all here

in a silent song

*It is not a desire
for object
or ego gain*

*It is a world
within its own
without malice or disdain*

*It is more than
just a presence
or mere space*

*It conveys
a deeper connection
a sense of life
of lasting influence
of a higher place*

We seek
the cool summer breezes
and calm release

We seek
the freedom of strength
nurtured at length

Whether it be
in happiness or pain
sunshine or rain

We seek the counsel
of cool summer breezes...
and calm release

He was a soothsayer they say
   who lived deep within
   the quite woods
   at the head of the bay

   He mingled in the lush
   forest glades so low
   and sat for hours
   along the soft river's flow

   He slept deep in the woods
   along silken creeks
   He walked through the meadows
   and the high craggy peaks

   His was a fate
   that pulled him so
   from the rumbling life
   we all have come to know

His convection was transparent
way beyond thought
within a struggling world
where we are often caught

They say this soothsayer
was part of the woods
the mountains and the sea

A person searching
for a deeper meaning
to be free

This solitary soothsayer
has now passed away...
but his spirit remains
at the head of the bay

His soul has become
part of the mountains
and the sea

Forever present
and forever free

Take a moment —

to reflect and see

Breathe slow

and deep...

as you become open

and become free...

"This view is **amazing**!"

"Ah…yes," he whispers,

"and you can see forever."

*D*istant mountains
        plains far below

Stillness...silence
        sheerness
                solitude

Vast eroded landscapes
        barren rock
            sand
                and soil

Fading sun
    evening glow
        cobalt sky
            lucent moon
                brilliant stars

Captivated
    mesmerized
        gazing
            absorbing

Inhaling
  slow
     long
        deep
           within...

                    Earth's skeleton
                        laid bare

                  A clarifying temple
                      for the mind

*Autumn days
bring warmth
of low-angle light*

*Golden shades
across the land
bring a humbling sight*

Alas —
 these days of glory
  soon will pass

  Fading from memory

   but etched deeply within
   a spirit that lasts

*T*wilight slides across the meadow
into the pine
heart beating in silence
slowing with time

    Down the river
    it blankets the land
    a darkening realm
    where the tree grove stands

    Disappearing into dusk...

        fading into

            silent
              light

*I*nto the quiet,

quiet

darkening night

May your breath

bring solace

like soft falling snow

With a comforting quiet

as the lamp

burns low

Minutes pass...
like shadows

evolving
transforming

Reflecting
    morphing
        into hours, days, seasons —
            years of life

    Perpetually moving
        steeping through
            moments of

            forgotten time

II

Pacific Inspiration

We come to this place

not knowing

all that we will become

We leave this place

humbled

inspired

forever changed

Wind-driven rain
 across my face
 tasting salt from the sea
 deep inside my body
 deep inside of me

Fresh Pacific air
    a refined sense of space
    inhaling sweetness from the sea
    deep inside my lungs
    deep inside of me

    Vast ocean horizons
        a poetry of place
        bringing solitude from the sea
        deep inside my mind
        deep inside of me

I have found
a quiet place

To view broad landscapes
and the sea

A mountainside
from which to think deeply
and to be free

A place to watch clouds mingle
and birds take wing

A calming place
where the nighttime sings

This is the place
my heart desires

A sacred place
for burning

my inner fires

"*Please grant me,
     just one more life.*

*Or maybe two,
     if you can…*

          please."

*H*ere lies a humble home
high on a hill
above the ocean
and the farm field till

Sit on the lanai
feel the day pass
gather your thoughts
make them last

The sun angles low
air so clear
soft evening sounds
bring music so dear

*Release the day
take a rest
do not struggle
reflect the best*

*Settle down
breathe so deep
these few hours
are dear to keep*

*Take it all in
do not seek
it is all here
as your thoughts
run deep*

Transcend...

clear the mind

*S*eek the core...

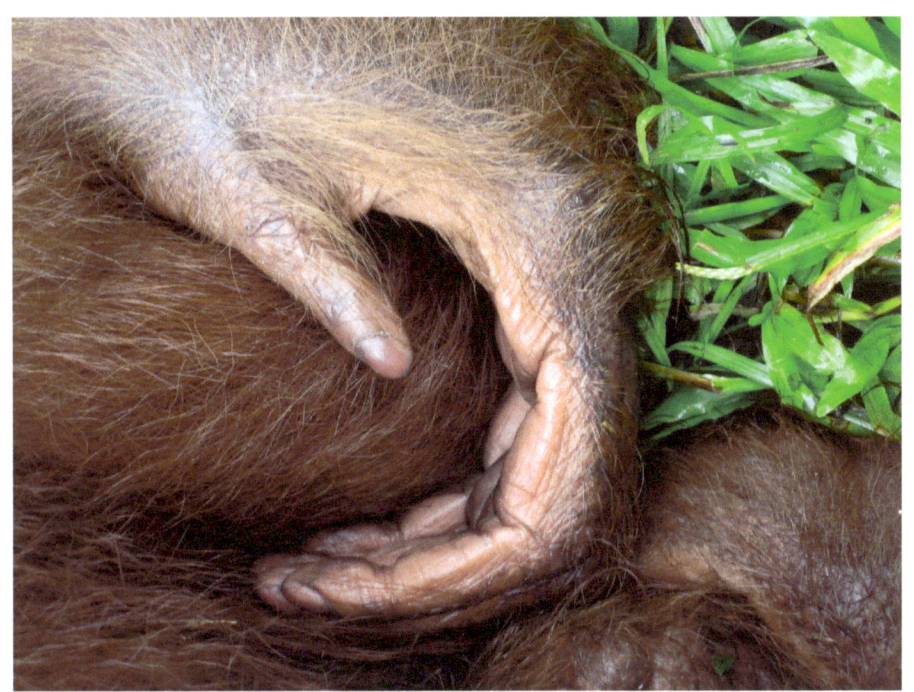

It was
this time

that brought
fine clarity

Of a far more rich
and complex
serenity

Quietly...
we move
homeward bound

With a slower pace
of awareness

searching
to be found

Stillness...

lingers...

in translucent

space

and time

III

Pursuing the Essence Within

*Deepest insights come
not in a rush*

*but in quiet moments
of a whispered hush*

*Inner perception
comes with time*

*through inner wisdom
and subtle sublime*

Sing the song
of perception and light

It is the soulful yearning
reaching for insight

Older is wiser,
as they say

When we slowly seek
the essence of each day

There are times and places

that some cannot live without.

These are some of those times...

WISDOM RUN | 79

To see the greatness of a mountain,
one must keep one's distance;

To understand its form,
one must move around it;

To experience its moods,
one must see it at sunrise and sunset,

At noon and at midnight,
in sun and in rain,

In snow and in storm,
in summer and in winter,
and in all the other seasons

He who can see the mountain like this
comes nearer to the life of the mountain.

— Lama Govinda

Good evening, my friend...

*This journey has gone well.
I have pushed my legs and my lungs
over many rugged, mountainous miles
on and on...for many long days*

*Working my body
opening my mind
in pristine
subalpine air*

*I slept long and deep
on distant ridges
with views so vast
and stars so near*

*I drank from
cold, pure streams
so fine
so clear*

*This sojourn has brought insights
of peaks, rivers, and glades,
verdant meadows and alpine lakes
with deep azure shades*

*I have freed myself from the tiring
lowland baggage and pace
seeing life anew
in this hollowed and cherished place*

*Soon I will leave these remarkable lands
and lose my strong, measured gait*

*yet bringing me lasting comfort
and a renewed sense of fate.*

Good night...

*S*equoias
at sunrise...

Another day
inhaling
growing

Since the pharaohs
they have been at it

one day
at a time

*Beginning
from a tiny seed*

*Nurtured in sun,
soil, water, air,
and space*

*They have grown
for millennia
into sentinels of time*

*It all may be simple, you see,
except if only you knew*

*the hundreds of
thousands of sunrises*

*that have quietly filtered into
these giant sequoia trees*

Old land

Simple land

Composition
texture
color

Artistry
of earth

*They have lived
for thousands of years*

The oldest that exist

*Limited water
harsh weather
poor soils
slow growth*

Yet, they survive —
    one day at a time

The secrets to old age —

    at least for some

Give me peace...

like a river

Seek
and ye shall find

the essence among

*changing light
and
limited time*

Nothing
so beautiful
can be found

within the
common hours of
preconceived thoughts

*Seek inspiration with
an open mind and heart*

*and the rewards
will be yours*

Journey

*to reach
into the stars*

Seek

*the missing pieces
that you have never known*

*You will understand
when they are
finally found*

Go
move, grow

*easily and freely
without hindrance or restraint*

To
knowledge
learning
evolution

Wisdom Run

www.ingramcontent.com/pod-product-compliance
Lightning Source LLC
Chambersburg PA
CBHW041802160426
43191CB00001B/6